CHARLESTON

Where History meets Hospitality

By

Boniface Hilz

About the Author

Boniface Hilz is a passionate traveler with a deep love for history and southern charm. Having explored countless destinations, Boniface Hilz has developed a keen eye for the unique details that make a place special.

Boniface Hilz believes that travel is about more than just sightseeing. It's about immersing oneself in local culture, savoring delicious cuisine, and connecting with people from all walks of life.

Whether you're a seasoned traveler or a first-time visitor, Boniface Hilz hopes this guide will inspire you to discover the beauty and history of Charleston.

Table of contents

QuickStart Guide

Top Sights

Charleston, South Carolina, a city steeped in history and brimming with Southern charm, offers a wealth of attractions for visitors. Here are some of the top sights to explore:

Historic Downtown Charleston

 * Rainbow Row: This iconic stretch of colorful Georgian row houses is a must-see for any visitor to Charleston. The pastel-hued homes, dating back to the 18th century, are a testament to the city's rich history and architectural beauty.

 * The Battery: Located at the southern tip of the peninsula, The Battery offers stunning views of Charleston Harbor and Fort Sumter. Take a leisurely stroll along the waterfront, admire the historic homes, and soak up the atmosphere of this historic district.

 * White Point Garden: This picturesque park, located adjacent to The Battery, is a popular spot

for picnics, people-watching, and enjoying the waterfront views.

 * French Quarter: This historic neighborhood is home to some of Charleston's most beautiful churches, including St. Michael's Episcopal Church and the French Huguenot Church.

 * King Street: This bustling street is a shopper's paradise, with a wide variety of boutiques, antique shops, and art galleries.
 * Charleston City Market: This historic market, housed in 19th-century buildings, is a great place to shop for local crafts, souvenirs, and fresh produce.

Plantations and Gardens
 * Magnolia Plantation and Gardens: This historic plantation, dating back to the 1670s, is renowned for its beautiful gardens, featuring a diverse array of plants and flowers.

 * Drayton Hall Plantation: This elegant plantation house, built in the Palladian style,

offers a glimpse into the lives of the South Carolina aristocracy.

 * Middleton Place Plantation: This historic plantation, known for its formal gardens and picturesque landscapes, is a popular destination for history buffs and nature lovers alike.

Museums and Cultural Attractions
 * The Charleston Museum: This museum, founded in 1773, is one of the oldest museums in the United States. It houses a diverse collection of artifacts, including art, historical documents, and natural history specimens.

 * Gibbes Museum of Art: This art museum, housed in a historic building, features a collection of American art from the 18th century to the present day.

 * Old Slave Mart Museum: This museum, located in a former slave market, tells the story of the transatlantic slave trade and its impact on Charleston.

* Nathaniel Russell House: This beautifully restored 18th-century mansion offers a glimpse into the lives of Charleston's elite.

Beaches and Outdoor Activities
* Folly Beach: This popular beach town, located just south of Charleston, offers great surfing, swimming, and sunbathing opportunities.

* Sullivan's Island: This historic island, known for its beautiful beaches and charming atmosphere, is a popular destination for families and couples.

* Isle of Palms: This barrier island, located just east of Charleston, offers pristine beaches, excellent fishing, and a variety of water sports.

Food and Drink
* Charleston Restaurant Scene: Charleston is home to a vibrant food scene, with a wide variety of restaurants offering everything from

traditional Southern cuisine to innovative fusion dishes.
 * Charleston Culinary Tours: Take a food tour to sample the city's best dishes and learn about its culinary history.
Events and Festivals
 * Spoleto Festival USA: This annual arts festival features a wide range of performances, including music, theater, dance, and visual arts.
 * Charleston Wine + Food Festival: This popular festival celebrates the best of Southern cuisine and wine.

Additional Tips
 * Best Time to Visit: The best time to visit Charleston is during the spring or fall, when the weather is mild and the crowds are smaller.
 * Getting Around: The best way to get around Charleston is on foot or by bike. There are also several bike-sharing programs available.
 * Accommodations: Charleston offers a wide variety of accommodations, from historic inns to modern hotels.

* Packing Tips: Be sure to pack comfortable walking shoes, sunscreen, and a hat.
Charleston is a city that offers something for everyone. Whether you're interested in history, culture, food, or outdoor activities, you're sure to find something to enjoy.

Local Life
Local life in Charleston is a delightful blend of Southern hospitality, rich history, and a laid-back coastal lifestyle. Here's a glimpse into what it's like to live in this charming city:
Daily Life
* Slow Pace: Charleston embraces a slower pace of life compared to many other American cities. Locals often prioritize quality time with family and friends over rushing through their days.

* Outdoor Activities: The mild climate allows for year-round outdoor activities. Residents enjoy spending time at the beach, biking, kayaking, and exploring the city's many parks and gardens.

* Community-Oriented: Charleston has a strong sense of community. Neighborhoods often host block parties, festivals, and other events that bring people together.
* Southern Hospitality: The city is renowned for its warm and welcoming atmosphere. Locals are known for their friendly demeanor and willingness to help visitors.

Social Scene
* Rooftop Bars: Charleston boasts a vibrant nightlife scene, with many rooftop bars offering stunning views of the city skyline and harbor.
* Live Music: The city has a thriving music scene, with live music performances at various venues throughout the week.
* Food and Drink: Charleston's culinary scene is world-class, with a wide variety of restaurants offering everything from traditional Southern cuisine to innovative fusion dishes.
* Farmers' Markets: Local farmers' markets provide fresh, seasonal produce and artisanal goods.

Culture and History
 * Historical Significance: Charleston is steeped in history, with many historic sites and landmarks dating back to the colonial era.
 * Art and Culture: The city has a vibrant arts scene, with numerous museums, galleries, and theaters.
 * Festivals and Events: Charleston hosts a variety of festivals and events throughout the year, including the Spoleto Festival USA and the Charleston Wine + Food Festival.

Tips for Living Like a Local
 * Explore the Neighborhoods: Venture beyond the historic district to discover the unique charm of different neighborhoods like West Ashley, Mount Pleasant, and Folly Beach.
 * Embrace the Local Cuisine: Try classic Lowcountry dishes like shrimp and grits, she-crab soup, and boiled peanuts.
 * Visit Local Businesses: Support local businesses by shopping at boutiques, dining at local restaurants, and attending community events.

* Take Advantage of Outdoor Activities: Enjoy the city's beautiful parks, beaches, and waterways.

Living in Charleston offers a unique blend of history, culture, and outdoor activities. By embracing the local lifestyle, you can truly experience the best of what this charming city has to offer.

Day Planner

A Charleston Day Planner

Here's a suggested itinerary for a day in Charleston:

Morning (9 AM - 12 PM)

* Historic Charleston Stroll: Begin your day by wandering through the historic district. Admire the colorful houses of Rainbow Row, the grand mansions of the French Quarter, and the serene beauty of White Point Garden.

* Breakfast at Husk: Indulge in a delicious Southern breakfast at Husk, a renowned restaurant that celebrates Lowcountry cuisine.

Afternoon (12 PM - 3 PM)

* Boat Tour: Take a harbor cruise to Fort Sumter, a significant historical site. Learn about the Civil War and enjoy panoramic views of the city skyline.
 * Lunch at Poe's Tavern: Enjoy a leisurely lunch at Poe's Tavern, a historic tavern with a charming atmosphere.
 * Shopping on King Street: Spend some time exploring the shops and boutiques on King Street, a popular shopping destination.
Evening (3 PM - 9 PM)
 * Plantation Tour: Visit a historic plantation like Drayton Hall or Middleton Place. Immerse yourself in the history of the antebellum South and admire the beautiful gardens.
 * Dinner at FIG: Enjoy a fine dining experience at FIG, a Michelin-starred restaurant known for its innovative cuisine.
 * Evening Stroll: Take a leisurely stroll through the historic district, admiring the illuminated buildings and the romantic atmosphere.

Additional Tips:

* Bike Rental: Consider renting a bike to explore the city at your own pace.
* Horse-Drawn Carriage Ride: Take a romantic horse-drawn carriage ride through the historic district.
* Ghost Tour: Experience the spooky side of Charleston with a ghost tour.
* Beach Day: If you have time, head to Folly Beach or Sullivan's Island for a day of sun, sand, and surf.

Remember to check specific opening hours and make reservations, especially for popular restaurants and attractions. Enjoy your time in Charleston!

Need to Know

Need to Know: Essential Information for Your Charleston Trip

Weather:
* Best Time to Visit: Spring (March-May) and Fall (September-November) are the most pleasant times to visit, with mild temperatures and lower humidity.

* Summer: Hot and humid, but perfect for beach days.
* Winter: Mild, with occasional cold fronts.
Currency:
* US Dollar: The US Dollar is widely accepted in Charleston.
Language:
* English: English is the primary language spoken.

Transportation:
* Walking: The historic district is best explored on foot.
* Biking: A great way to get around, with bike rental shops available.
* Car Rental: Useful for exploring the surrounding areas and beaches.
* Public Transportation: Limited options, but the CARTA bus system serves the city.
Tipping:
* Restaurants: 15-20% tip is customary.
* Bars: A dollar or two per drink is standard.
* Taxis and Rideshares: 15-20% tip is common.
Safety:

* Charleston is generally safe, but like any city, it's wise to take precautions, especially at night.

* Be aware of your surroundings, especially in crowded areas.

Etiquette:

* Southern Hospitality: Locals are known for their friendly and welcoming nature.

* Dress Code: While Charleston has a casual atmosphere, dressing modestly is generally appreciated, especially in historical sites and churches.

Emergency Numbers:
 * Police: 911
Local Customs:
 * Sweet Tea: A Southern staple, often served iced.
 * Lowcountry Cuisine: Try local delicacies like shrimp and grits, she-crab soup, and boiled peanuts.
 * Historical Significance: Respect the city's rich history and heritage.
By keeping these tips in mind, you can make the most of your Charleston experience.

Charleston Neighborhoods
Charleston offers a diverse range of neighborhoods, each with its own unique charm and character. Here are some of the most popular neighborhoods:
Peninsula Neighborhoods:
 * French Quarter: Known for its historic charm, cobblestone streets, and elegant architecture.

* Harleston Village: A vibrant neighborhood with a mix of historic homes and modern condos.

* South of Broad: A prestigious neighborhood with stunning waterfront views and grand mansions.

* Cannonborough-Elliotborough: A trendy neighborhood with a mix of historic homes, art galleries, and boutiques.

* Mazyck-Wraggborough: A charming neighborhood with a mix of historic homes and modern condos.

* Ansonborough: A historic neighborhood with a mix of historic homes and modern condos.

Other Notable Neighborhoods:
* Daniel Island: A master-planned community with a mix of residential and commercial development.

* Mount Pleasant: A popular suburb with a mix of residential and commercial development.

* West Ashley: A diverse neighborhood with a mix of residential and commercial development.

* James Island: A historic island with a mix of residential and commercial development.

* Folly Beach: A popular beach town with a laid-back atmosphere.

* Isle of Palms: A barrier island with beautiful beaches and a variety of recreational activities.

Additional Tips:
* The best neighborhood for you will depend on your individual needs and preferences.
* Consider your budget, lifestyle, and desired amenities when choosing a neighborhood.
* Do your research and visit different neighborhoods to get a feel for the atmosphere.
* Talk to local residents to get their insights and recommendations.

By doing your research and considering your individual needs, you can find the perfect Charleston neighborhood for you.

Explore
Exploring Charleston's Historic Charm and Coastal Beauty
Charleston, South Carolina, is a city steeped in history, culture, and natural beauty. With its cobblestone streets, historic architecture, and stunning waterfront, Charleston offers a unique and unforgettable experience. Here are some of the must-see attractions and activities:
Historic Downtown Charleston
 * Rainbow Row: A vibrant row of colorful Georgian houses that is iconic to Charleston.

 * The Battery: A picturesque waterfront promenade with stunning views of Charleston Harbor.

 * French Quarter: A historic neighborhood with charming streets and beautiful churches.

* King Street: A bustling street lined with shops, boutiques, and restaurants.
* Charleston City Market: A historic market where you can find local crafts, souvenirs, and fresh produce.

Plantations and Gardens
* Magnolia Plantation and Gardens: A historic plantation with beautiful gardens and a diverse array of plants and flowers.

* Drayton Hall Plantation: A well-preserved plantation house that offers a glimpse into the lives of the South Carolina aristocracy.

* Middleton Place Plantation: A historic plantation known for its formal gardens and picturesque landscapes.

Museums and Cultural Attractions
* The Charleston Museum: One of the oldest museums in the United States, featuring a diverse collection of artifacts.

* Gibbes Museum of Art: A renowned art museum showcasing American art from the 18th century to the present.

* Old Slave Mart Museum: A poignant museum that tells the story of the transatlantic slave trade.

* Nathaniel Russell House: A beautifully restored 18th-century mansion.

Beaches and Outdoor Activities
* Folly Beach: A popular beach town with great surfing, swimming, and sunbathing opportunities.

* Sullivan's Island: A historic island with beautiful beaches and a charming atmosphere.

* Isle of Palms: A barrier island with pristine beaches, excellent fishing, and water sports.

Food and Drink
* Charleston Restaurant Scene: A vibrant food scene with a wide variety of restaurants offering

everything from traditional Southern cuisine to innovative fusion dishes.

* Charleston Culinary Tours: Take a food tour to sample the city's best dishes and learn about its culinary history.

Events and Festivals

* Spoleto Festival USA: A renowned arts festival featuring music, theater, dance, and visual arts.

* Charleston Wine + Food Festival: A popular festival celebrating the best of Southern cuisine and wine.

Tips for Exploring Charleston:

* Best Time to Visit: Spring and Fall are the most pleasant times to visit, with mild temperatures and lower humidity.

* Getting Around: The best way to get around the historic district is on foot. Consider renting a bike or taking a horse-drawn carriage ride.

* Accommodations: Charleston offers a wide variety of accommodations, from historic inns to modern hotels.

* Packing Tips: Pack comfortable walking shoes, sunscreen, and a hat.

By following these tips, you can make the most of your time in Charleston and experience all the city has to offer.

Historic Downtown Charleston

Historic Downtown Charleston

Historic Downtown Charleston is a captivating blend of Southern charm, rich history, and stunning architecture. Here's a glimpse into this enchanting district:

Key Attractions:
* Rainbow Row: A picturesque row of pastel-colored Georgian houses, a must-see for any visitor.

* The Battery: A serene waterfront park offering stunning views of Charleston Harbor and Fort Sumter.

* French Quarter: A historic neighborhood with charming streets, beautiful churches, and elegant mansions.

* King Street: A bustling shopping street lined with boutiques, antique stores, and art galleries.
* Charleston City Market: A vibrant market offering local crafts, souvenirs, and fresh produce.

Things to Do:
* Horse-Drawn Carriage Tours: Experience the city's history and charm on a leisurely carriage ride.

* Ghost Tours: Embark on a spooky adventure through the city's haunted streets.
* Plantation Tours: Visit nearby plantations like Drayton Hall and Middleton Place to learn about the antebellum South.
* Food Tours: Savor the flavors of Charleston's culinary scene on a guided food tour.
* Water Tours: Take a boat tour to Fort Sumter or explore the waterways around Charleston.
* Museum Visits: Immerse yourself in the city's history at the Charleston Museum or the Gibbes Museum of Art.

Tips for Exploring Historic Downtown Charleston:
* Best Time to Visit: Spring and Fall offer pleasant weather and fewer crowds.

* Comfortable Shoes: Wear comfortable shoes for exploring the cobblestone streets.
* Hydrate: Stay hydrated, especially during the warmer months.
* Respectful Dress: Dress modestly, especially when visiting churches and historical sites.
* Plan Ahead: Research attractions and make reservations for popular restaurants.

By exploring Historic Downtown Charleston, you'll be transported back in time and experience the timeless beauty of this Southern gem.

King Street

King Street is a premier shopping and dining destination in Charleston, South Carolina. It's a vibrant and historic street that offers a unique blend of local boutiques, national brands, and renowned restaurants.

Shopping on King Street:
* Local Boutiques: Discover unique finds and Southern charm at local boutiques like Hampden Clothing, M. Dumas & Sons, and Iva Jean.

* National Brands: Indulge in retail therapy at stores like Lululemon, Anthropologie, and Tory Burch.
* Antique Shops: Explore the treasures of the past at antique shops like George C. Birlant & Co.

Dining on King Street:
* Fine Dining: Enjoy exquisite cuisine at restaurants like Husk, FIG, and Halls Chophouse.
* Casual Dining: Grab a bite to eat at popular spots like Rodney Scott's BBQ and Slightly North of Broad.
* Coffee Shops: Sip on your favorite beverage at local coffee shops like Kudu Coffee and The Daily.

Other Attractions on King Street:
* Historic Architecture: Admire the beautiful architecture of the historic buildings lining King Street.

* Art Galleries: Discover local and international art at galleries like Jonathan Green Gallery and William Aiken Gallery.
 * Live Music: Enjoy live music at various bars and restaurants along King Street.
Whether you're a shopaholic, a foodie, or simply looking to explore the city's vibrant culture, King Street has something for everyone.

The French Quarter
The French Quarter in Charleston, South Carolina, is a charming and historic neighborhood known for its beautiful architecture, cobblestone streets, and rich history.
Key Attractions:
 * French Huguenot Church: This beautiful Gothic Revival church is one of the oldest Protestant congregations in the United States.

 * St. Philip's Episcopal Church: This historic church features stunning stained glass windows and a beautiful cemetery.

* Old Slave Mart Museum: This museum tells the story of the transatlantic slave trade and its impact on Charleston.

* Dock Street Theatre: This historic theater is one of the oldest in the United States and still hosts performances today.
* Charleston City Market: This vibrant market offers a variety of local crafts, souvenirs, and fresh produce.

Things to Do:
* Stroll through the historic streets: Take a leisurely stroll through the neighborhood and admire the beautiful architecture.
* Visit the museums and churches: Learn about the history and culture of Charleston.
* Shop at the boutiques and galleries: Find unique souvenirs and gifts.
* Dine at the restaurants: Enjoy delicious Southern cuisine at one of the many restaurants in the French Quarter.
* Take a carriage ride: Experience the charm of Charleston from a horse-drawn carriage.

Tips for Visiting the French Quarter:
 * Best Time to Visit: Spring and Fall are the most pleasant times to visit, with mild temperatures and fewer crowds.
 * Comfortable Shoes: Wear comfortable shoes, as the streets can be uneven.
 * Hydrate: Stay hydrated, especially during the warmer months.
 * Respectful Dress: Dress modestly, especially when visiting churches and historical sites.
 * Plan Ahead: Research attractions and make reservations for popular restaurants.
The French Quarter is a must-see for any visitor to Charleston. With its rich history, beautiful architecture, and vibrant atmosphere, it is sure to leave a lasting impression.

The Battery
The Battery in Charleston, South Carolina, is a historic seawall and promenade that offers stunning views of Charleston Harbor and its surrounding landmarks.
Key Features:

* Historic Architecture: The Battery is lined with beautiful antebellum houses, each with its own unique history and architectural style.

* White Point Garden: This picturesque park is located across the street from The Battery and offers a peaceful escape with lush greenery and beautiful views.

* Waterfront Views: Enjoy panoramic views of Charleston Harbor, including Fort Sumter, Fort Moultrie, and Sullivan's Island.
* Walking Paths: The Battery provides a scenic walking path perfect for leisurely strolls or morning jogs.

Things to Do:
* Stroll along the seawall: Take in the stunning views of the harbor and admire the historic architecture.
* Visit White Point Garden: Relax in the serene park and enjoy the beautiful scenery.
* People-watch: Observe locals and tourists alike as they enjoy the waterfront.

* Photograph the scenery: Capture the beauty of Charleston's skyline and the historic houses.
* Picnic: Pack a picnic lunch and enjoy a meal with a view.

Tips for Visiting The Battery:
* Best Time to Visit: Early morning or late afternoon are ideal times to avoid crowds and enjoy the peaceful atmosphere.
* Comfortable Shoes: Wear comfortable shoes for walking along the seawall.
* Sunscreen and Hat: Protect yourself from the sun, especially during the summer months.
* Camera: Bring a camera to capture the stunning views and historic architecture.
* Respect the Environment: Please respect the natural beauty of the area by keeping it clean and free of litter.

The Battery is a must-visit destination for anyone exploring Charleston. Its combination of history, natural beauty, and peaceful atmosphere make it a truly special place.

Rainbow Row

Rainbow Row is a series of thirteen colorful historic houses located on East Bay Street in Charleston, South Carolina. It's one of the most photographed spots in the city, known for its vibrant pastel hues.

History:

 * Originally built in the mid-18th century, these homes were part of a bustling commercial area.

 * After the Civil War, the neighborhood fell into disrepair.

 * In the 1930s and 1940s, the houses were restored and painted in their iconic pastel colors.

Why the Colorful Paint Scheme?

There are several theories about the reason for the colorful paint scheme:

 * To attract sailors: Some believe the bright colors were used to help drunken sailors find their way back to their lodgings.

 * To identify different stores: Others suggest that the colors were used to help illiterate slaves identify different shops when the houses were used as commercial buildings.

* Aesthetic appeal: Simply to make the row of houses more visually appealing.

Today:
 * Rainbow Row is a popular tourist destination, attracting visitors from all over the world.
 * The houses are privately owned, so they are not open to the public.
 * However, you can still admire their beauty from the street or take a guided tour.

Tips for Visiting Rainbow Row:
 * Best Time to Visit: Early morning or late afternoon are ideal times to avoid crowds and capture the best lighting for photos.
 * Photography: Bring your camera to capture the vibrant colors and historic architecture.
 * Respectful Viewing: Please be mindful of the residents and avoid disturbing their privacy.
 * Guided Tours: Consider taking a guided tour to learn more about the history and architecture of Rainbow Row.

Rainbow Row is a must-see attraction in Charleston, offering a glimpse into the city's rich history and colorful culture.

Sullivan's Island
Sullivan's Island is a charming coastal town located just outside of Charleston, South Carolina. Known for its beautiful beaches, rich history, and laid-back atmosphere, it's a popular destination for both locals and tourists.
Key Attractions:
 * Fort Moultrie: This historic fort played a crucial role in the American Revolution and the Civil War. Visitors can explore the fort, learn about its history, and enjoy stunning views of the harbor.

 * Sullivan's Island Beach: The island's pristine beaches offer opportunities for swimming, sunbathing, and surfing. The beach is also known for its strong currents, so it's important to swim with caution.

* Sullivan's Island Lighthouse: This iconic lighthouse, built in 1962, is one of the most modern lighthouses in the United States.

* Edgar Allan Poe Connection: Edgar Allan Poe was stationed at Fort Moultrie in the 1820s, and the island served as the inspiration for his short story "The Gold Bug."

Things to Do:
* Beach Activities: Enjoy swimming, sunbathing, surfing, and beachcombing.
* History Exploration: Visit Fort Moultrie and learn about its significant role in American history.
* Dining: Savor delicious seafood and other local cuisine at the island's many restaurants.
* Shopping: Browse unique shops and boutiques for souvenirs and local products.
* Birdwatching: Keep an eye out for a variety of bird species, including migratory birds and seabirds.

Tips for Visiting Sullivan's Island:

* Best Time to Visit: Spring and Fall offer pleasant weather and fewer crowds.
* Beach Safety: Be aware of the strong currents and swim only in designated areas.
* Parking: Parking can be limited, especially during peak season. Consider arriving early or using public transportation.
* Sun Protection: Apply sunscreen and wear a hat to protect yourself from the sun.
* Respect the Environment: Keep the beaches clean and dispose of trash properly.
Sullivan's Island offers a relaxing and unforgettable experience, combining history, nature, and coastal charm.

Folly Beach

Folly Beach, often referred to as "The Edge of America," is a charming coastal town located just south of Charleston, South Carolina. Known for its laid-back atmosphere, beautiful beaches, and vibrant surf culture, Folly Beach offers a unique experience for visitors of all ages.
Key Attractions:

* Folly Beach Pier: This iconic pier stretches over the Atlantic Ocean, offering stunning views and opportunities for fishing.

* The Washout: A popular surfing spot known for its strong waves and challenging breaks.
* Center Street: This lively street is lined with shops, restaurants, and bars, offering a variety of dining and entertainment options.
* Folly Beach County Park: This park offers picnic areas, a playground, and a nature trail.
* Lighthouse Inlet Heritage Preserve: This preserve offers beautiful views of Morris Island Lighthouse and a variety of wildlife.

Things to Do:
* Beach Activities: Enjoy swimming, sunbathing, surfing, and beachcombing.
* Water Sports: Try your hand at kayaking, paddleboarding, or fishing.
* Dining: Savor delicious seafood and other local cuisine at the many restaurants and bars.
* Shopping: Browse unique shops and boutiques for souvenirs and local products.

* Wildlife Watching: Keep an eye out for dolphins, sea turtles, and a variety of bird species.

Tips for Visiting Folly Beach:
 * Best Time to Visit: Spring and Fall offer pleasant weather and fewer crowds.
 * Beach Safety: Be aware of the strong currents and swim only in designated areas.
 * Parking: Parking can be limited, especially during peak season. Consider arriving early or using public transportation.
 * Sun Protection: Apply sunscreen and wear a hat to protect yourself from the sun.
 * Respect the Environment: Keep the beaches clean and dispose of trash properly.
Folly Beach is a perfect destination for those seeking a relaxing and fun-filled beach vacation. With its laid-back atmosphere, stunning beaches, and vibrant community, Folly Beach offers something for everyone.

Mount Pleasant

Mount Pleasant is a charming town located just across the Cooper River from Charleston, South Carolina. Known for its beautiful waterfront, historic sites, and family-friendly atmosphere, Mount Pleasant offers a variety of activities and attractions for visitors of all ages.

Key Attractions:

* Patriots Point Naval & Maritime Museum: This museum features the USS Yorktown aircraft carrier, the USS Claxton destroyer, and the USS Laffey destroyer.

* Shem Creek: This picturesque waterfront area offers a variety of restaurants, bars, and shops. It's a popular spot for dining, drinking, and people-watching.

* Mount Pleasant Waterfront Park: This beautiful park offers stunning views of the Charleston Harbor, a playground, a fishing pier, and a dog park.

* Old Village: This historic district features charming homes, churches, and shops.

* Sullivan's Island: This nearby island offers beautiful beaches, historic sites, and a laid-back atmosphere.

Things to Do:
 * Explore Patriots Point Naval & Maritime Museum: Learn about naval history and climb aboard historic ships.
 * Dine at Shem Creek: Enjoy delicious seafood and other local cuisine at one of the many restaurants.
 * Relax at Mount Pleasant Waterfront Park: Take a leisurely stroll, have a picnic, or fish from the pier.
 * Shop in the Old Village: Browse unique boutiques and antique shops.
 * Visit Sullivan's Island: Spend a day at the beach, visit Fort Moultrie, or explore the island's historic district.

Tips for Visiting Mount Pleasant:
 * Best Time to Visit: Spring and Fall offer pleasant weather and fewer crowds.

* Parking: Parking can be limited in some areas, especially during peak season.
* Sun Protection: Apply sunscreen and wear a hat to protect yourself from the sun.
* Respect the Environment: Keep the beaches and parks clean and dispose of trash properly. Mount Pleasant is a great place to experience the beauty and charm of the Charleston area. With its diverse attractions, friendly locals, and laid-back atmosphere, it's a perfect destination for a relaxing getaway.

Kiawah Island

Kiawah Island is a luxurious barrier island located just 25 miles southwest of Charleston, South Carolina. Known for its pristine beaches, world-class golf courses, and serene natural beauty, Kiawah Island offers a tranquil and upscale escape.

Key Features:

 * Kiawah Island Golf Resort: This prestigious resort boasts five championship golf courses designed by renowned architects like Pete Dye and Tom Fazio. The Ocean Course on Kiawah Island has hosted major golf tournaments, including the PGA Championship.

 * Miles of Pristine Beaches: The island offers 10 miles of unspoiled beaches with soft sand and gentle waves, perfect for swimming, sunbathing, and shelling.

 * Nature and Wildlife: Kiawah Island is home to a diverse ecosystem, including marshes, maritime forests, and a variety of wildlife.

Visitors can enjoy birdwatching, kayaking, and other outdoor activities.
 * The Sanctuary at Kiawah Island: This luxurious resort hotel offers world-class accommodations, dining, and spa services.

Things to Do:
 * Golf: Play a round of golf on one of the island's championship courses.
 * Beach Activities: Enjoy swimming, sunbathing, and beachcombing.
 * Nature Exploration: Hike or bike the island's trails, kayak through the marshes, or go birdwatching.
 * Spa and Wellness: Relax and rejuvenate at the resort's spa.
 * Dining: Savor delicious cuisine at the resort's restaurants, from casual fare to fine dining.

Tips for Visiting Kiawah Island:
 * Best Time to Visit: Spring and Fall offer pleasant weather and fewer crowds.

* Reservations: Book accommodations and activities in advance, especially during peak season.

* Dress Code: While the island has a relaxed atmosphere, some restaurants and activities may have a dress code.

* Respect the Environment: Keep the beaches and natural areas clean and avoid disturbing wildlife.

* Golf Cart Rentals: Consider renting a golf cart to explore the island.

Kiawah Island offers a luxurious and serene escape for those seeking a relaxing and rejuvenating vacation. With its pristine beaches, world-class golf courses, and natural beauty, Kiawah Island is a true paradise.

Seabrook Island

Seabrook Island is a private, gated barrier island located in Charleston County, South Carolina. Known for its pristine beaches, lush maritime forests, and a variety of outdoor activities, Seabrook Island offers a tranquil and upscale escape.

Key Features:
 * Miles of Pristine Beaches: The island boasts miles of beautiful beaches, perfect for swimming, sunbathing, and shelling.
 * The Seabrook Island Club: This private club offers a variety of amenities, including golf courses, tennis courts, a fitness center, and swimming pools.
 * Maritime Forest: Explore the island's lush maritime forest, home to a diverse array of wildlife.
 * Birdwatching: Seabrook Island is a birdwatcher's paradise, with numerous species of birds inhabiting the island's forests and marshes.
 * Water Activities: Enjoy kayaking, paddleboarding, and fishing in the surrounding waterways.

Things to Do:
 * Beach Activities: Relax on the beach, swim in the ocean, or build sandcastles.
 * Golf: Play a round of golf on one of the island's championship courses.

* Tennis: Enjoy a game of tennis on one of the club's well-maintained courts.
* Nature Exploration: Hike or bike through the island's trails, kayak through the marshes, or go birdwatching.
* Spa and Wellness: Relax and rejuvenate at the club's spa.
* Dining: Savor delicious cuisine at the island's restaurants, from casual fare to fine dining.

Tips for Visiting Seabrook Island:
* Access: Seabrook Island is a private community, so you'll need to be a guest of a resident or stay at one of the island's accommodations.
* Best Time to Visit: Spring and Fall offer pleasant weather and fewer crowds.
* Respect the Environment: Keep the beaches and natural areas clean and avoid disturbing wildlife.
* Golf Cart Rentals: Consider renting a golf cart to explore the island.
Seabrook Island offers a luxurious and serene escape for those seeking a relaxing and

rejuvenating vacation. With its pristine beaches, world-class amenities, and natural beauty, Seabrook Island is a true paradise.

Isle of Palms
The Isle of Palms is a beautiful barrier island located just north of Charleston, South Carolina. Known for its pristine beaches, calm waters, and laid-back atmosphere, it's a popular destination for families and beach lovers.

Key Attractions:
 * Isle of Palms County Park: This expansive park offers a variety of amenities, including a beach, picnic areas, a playground, and a fishing pier.
 * Wild Dunes Resort: This luxurious resort offers world-class golf courses, tennis courts, a spa, and a variety of dining options.
 * The Beach: With miles of white sandy beaches, the Isle of Palms is perfect for sunbathing, swimming, and building sandcastles.

* Water Sports: Enjoy kayaking, paddleboarding, surfing, and fishing in the surrounding waters.

Things to Do:
* Beach Activities: Relax on the beach, swim in the ocean, or build sandcastles.
* Golf: Play a round of golf on one of the island's championship courses.
* Tennis: Enjoy a game of tennis at the Wild Dunes Resort.
* Spa and Wellness: Relax and rejuvenate at the resort's spa.
* Dining: Savor delicious seafood and other local cuisine at the island's restaurants.
* Shopping: Browse unique shops and boutiques for souvenirs and local products.

Tips for Visiting the Isle of Palms:
* Best Time to Visit: Spring and Fall offer pleasant weather and fewer crowds.
* Beach Safety: Be aware of the tides and currents, and swim only in designated areas.

* Parking: Parking can be limited, especially during peak season. Consider arriving early or using public transportation.
 * Sun Protection: Apply sunscreen and wear a hat to protect yourself from the sun.
 * Respect the Environment: Keep the beaches and natural areas clean and avoid disturbing wildlife.
The Isle of Palms is a perfect destination for a relaxing beach vacation. With its beautiful beaches, calm waters, and variety of activities, it's a great place to unwind and enjoy the coastal lifestyle.

Best
The "best" things to do in Charleston are subjective and depend on your personal interests. However, here are some of the top-rated attractions and activities that consistently receive high praise:
Must-See Attractions:
 * Historic Downtown Charleston: Explore the charming streets, admire the colorful houses of

Rainbow Row, and visit historic sites like the French Quarter and The Battery.
 * Charleston City Market: Immerse yourself in the vibrant atmosphere of this historic market, where you can find local crafts, souvenirs, and fresh produce.

 * Fort Sumter and Fort Moultrie: Take a boat tour to these historic forts and learn about their role in American history.

 * Magnolia Plantation and Gardens: Wander through the beautiful gardens and learn about the history of this antebellum plantation.

 * Drayton Hall Plantation: Explore this well-preserved plantation house and its surrounding grounds.

Outdoor Activities:
 * Beaches: Relax on the pristine beaches of Folly Beach, Sullivan's Island, or Isle of Palms.

* Boating and Water Sports: Enjoy kayaking, paddleboarding, or fishing in the Charleston Harbor.
* Hiking and Biking: Explore the natural beauty of the area on foot or by bike.

Cultural Experiences:
* Museums: Visit the Charleston Museum, the Gibbes Museum of Art, or the International African American Museum.
* Food Tours: Sample the delicious cuisine of Charleston on a food tour.
* Live Music: Enjoy live music at one of the many bars and music venues.

Additional Tips:
* Best Time to Visit: Spring and Fall offer pleasant weather and fewer crowds.
* Transportation: Consider renting a car or using public transportation to get around.
* Accommodations: Book your accommodations in advance, especially during peak season.

* Budget: Charleston can be a bit pricey, but there are plenty of affordable options available. No matter what your interests are, you're sure to find something to enjoy in Charleston.

The Best of Charleston.
The Best of Charleston: A Guide to the Holy City
Charleston, South Carolina, is a city steeped in history, culture, and Southern charm. Here are some of the best things to do and see in this enchanting city:
Historic Downtown Charleston
 * Rainbow Row: A vibrant row of colorful Georgian houses that is iconic to Charleston.

 * The Battery: A picturesque waterfront promenade with stunning views of Charleston Harbor.

 * French Quarter: A historic neighborhood with charming streets, beautiful churches, and elegant mansions.

* King Street: A bustling street lined with shops, boutiques, and restaurants.
* Charleston City Market: A historic market where you can find local crafts, souvenirs, and fresh produce.

Plantations and Gardens
* Magnolia Plantation and Gardens: A historic plantation with beautiful gardens and a diverse array of plants and flowers.

* Drayton Hall Plantation: A well-preserved plantation house that offers a glimpse into the lives of the South Carolina aristocracy.

* Middleton Place Plantation: A historic plantation known for its formal gardens and picturesque landscapes.

Museums and Cultural Attractions
* The Charleston Museum: One of the oldest museums in the United States, featuring a diverse collection of artifacts.

* Gibbes Museum of Art: A renowned art museum showcasing American art from the 18th century to the present.

* Old Slave Mart Museum: A poignant museum that tells the story of the transatlantic slave trade.

* Nathaniel Russell House: A beautifully restored 18th-century mansion.

Beaches and Outdoor Activities
* Folly Beach: A popular beach town with great surfing, swimming, and sunbathing opportunities.

* Sullivan's Island: A historic island with beautiful beaches and a charming atmosphere.

* Isle of Palms: A barrier island with pristine beaches, excellent fishing, and water sports.

Food and Drink
* Charleston Restaurant Scene: A vibrant food scene with a wide variety of restaurants offering

everything from traditional Southern cuisine to innovative fusion dishes.

 * Charleston Culinary Tours: Take a food tour to sample the city's best dishes and learn about its culinary history.

Events and Festivals

 * Spoleto Festival USA: A renowned arts festival featuring music, theater, dance, and visual arts.

 * Charleston Wine + Food Festival: A popular festival celebrating the best of Southern cuisine and wine.

Tips for Exploring Charleston:

 * Best Time to Visit: Spring and Fall are the most pleasant times to visit, with mild temperatures and lower humidity.

 * Getting Around: The best way to get around the historic district is on foot. Consider renting a bike or taking a horse-drawn carriage ride.

 * Accommodations: Charleston offers a wide variety of accommodations, from historic inns to modern hotels.

* Packing Tips: Pack comfortable walking shoes, sunscreen, and a hat.

By following these tips and exploring the city's many attractions, you can experience the best of Charleston and create unforgettable memories.

Historic Charleston

Historic Charleston: A Journey Through Time Charleston, South Carolina, is a city steeped in history, with its charming streets, beautiful architecture, and rich cultural heritage. Here's a glimpse into the historical side of this enchanting city:

Must-Visit Historic Sites:

* Rainbow Row: A vibrant row of colorful Georgian houses, iconic to Charleston.

* The Battery: A serene waterfront promenade offering stunning views of Charleston Harbor and Fort Sumter.

* French Quarter: A historic neighborhood with charming streets, beautiful churches, and elegant mansions.

* King Street: A bustling street lined with shops, boutiques, and restaurants.
* Charleston City Market: A historic market offering local crafts, souvenirs, and fresh produce.

* Fort Sumter: This historic fort is where the Civil War began. It's accessible by boat tour.

* Fort Moultrie: Another significant historical fort, played a key role in the American Revolution and Civil War.

Historical Experiences:
* Horse-Drawn Carriage Tours: Experience the city's history and charm on a leisurely carriage ride.
* Ghost Tours: Embark on a spooky adventure through the city's haunted streets.
* Plantation Tours: Visit nearby plantations like Drayton Hall and Middleton Place to learn about the antebellum South.

* Museum Visits: Immerse yourself in the city's history at the Charleston Museum or the Gibbes Museum of Art.

Tips for Exploring Historic Charleston:
* Best Time to Visit: Spring and Fall offer pleasant weather and fewer crowds.
* Comfortable Shoes: Wear comfortable shoes for exploring the cobblestone streets.
* Hydrate: Stay hydrated, especially during the warmer months.
* Respectful Dress: Dress modestly, especially when visiting churches and historical sites.
* Plan Ahead: Research attractions and make reservations for popular restaurants.
By exploring Historic Downtown Charleston, you'll be transported back in time and experience the timeless beauty of this Southern gem.

Modern Charleston

While Charleston is renowned for its rich history and charming old-world charm, it also boasts a vibrant and modern side. Here's a glimpse into the contemporary face of Charleston:

A Fusion of Old and New:
 * Modern Architecture: Amidst the historic buildings, you'll find sleek, contemporary structures that blend seamlessly with the city's traditional architecture.

 * Art and Culture: Charleston has a thriving arts scene, with numerous art galleries, museums, and cultural events showcasing both traditional and contemporary works.
 * Foodie Paradise: Charleston's culinary scene is a fusion of classic Southern cuisine and innovative modern flavors. You'll find a wide range of restaurants, from casual eateries to Michelin-starred establishments.

 * Craft Beer and Cocktail Culture: The city boasts a growing craft beer scene, with breweries offering unique and flavorful brews. Additionally, Charleston has a thriving cocktail culture, with mixologists crafting innovative drinks.
A Thriving Community:

* Young Professionals: Charleston has attracted a growing number of young professionals who are drawn to the city's vibrant culture, job opportunities, and outdoor lifestyle.

 * Diverse Neighborhoods: The city offers a variety of neighborhoods, from historic districts to modern developments, catering to different lifestyles and preferences.
 * Community Events: Charleston hosts a variety of community events throughout the year, including festivals, farmers' markets, and cultural celebrations.
Outdoor Lifestyle:
 * Waterfront Activities: Charleston's waterfront offers opportunities for kayaking, paddleboarding, sailing, and fishing.

 * Parks and Green Spaces: The city has numerous parks and green spaces, perfect for picnics, jogging, and outdoor recreation.
 * Beach Life: Charleston's nearby beaches, such as Folly Beach, Sullivan's Island, and Isle of

Palms, offer opportunities for sunbathing, swimming, and surfing.

Charleston's unique blend of history and modernity makes it a captivating city for people of all ages. Whether you're interested in exploring its rich history, indulging in its culinary delights, or enjoying its outdoor activities, Charleston has something to offer.

Tours
Charleston offers a variety of tours to explore its rich history, beautiful architecture, and vibrant culture. Here are some of the most popular tours: Historical Tours:
 * Horse-drawn Carriage Tours: Experience the city's charm and history from a leisurely carriage ride.
 * Walking Tours: Explore the historic district on foot, learning about the city's past and present.

 * Ghost Tours: Embark on a spooky adventure through the city's haunted streets and cemeteries.

* Plantation Tours: Visit nearby plantations like Drayton Hall and Middleton Place to learn about the antebellum South.

Boat Tours:

* Harbor Cruises: Enjoy scenic views of Charleston Harbor, Fort Sumter, and the city skyline.

* Dolphin Watching Cruises: Spot dolphins and other marine life in their natural habitat.

* Fort Sumter Tours: Take a boat tour to Fort Sumter, the site of the first shots of the Civil War.

Food Tours:

* Food Walking Tours: Sample delicious local cuisine and learn about Charleston's culinary history.

* Cooking Classes: Learn how to prepare Southern dishes from local chefs.

Other Unique Tours:

* Bicycle Tours: Explore the city on two wheels, covering more ground and enjoying the fresh air.

* Segway Tours: A fun and unique way to see the city.
* Kayak Tours: Paddle through the city's waterways and enjoy stunning views.

Where to Book Tours:
* Online Tour Operators: Websites like Viator, GetYourGuide, and TripAdvisor offer a variety of tours and activities.
* Local Tour Companies: Bulldog Tours, Charleston Strolls, and Charleston Harbor Tours are some of the popular local tour companies.
* Your Hotel: Many hotels in Charleston offer concierge services that can help you book tours and activities.

By taking a tour, you can gain a deeper understanding of Charleston's history, culture, and natural beauty. Whether you're interested in history, food, or outdoor activities, there's a tour for you.

Festivals

Charleston hosts a variety of festivals throughout the year, celebrating its rich history, culture, and culinary delights. Here are some of the most popular festivals:

Annual Festivals:

* Spoleto Festival USA: A world-renowned performing arts festival featuring music, theater, dance, and visual arts.

* MOJA Arts Festival: A celebration of African and Caribbean culture, featuring music, dance, art, and food.

* Charleston Wine + Food Festival: A culinary extravaganza showcasing the best of Southern cuisine and wine.

* Southeastern Wildlife Exposition: A premier wildlife art show and sporting event.

* Charleston International Film Festival: A showcase of independent films from around the world.

* Family Circle Cup: A professional women's tennis tournament.

* Lowcountry Oyster Festival: A celebration of all things oysters, featuring oyster roasts, cooking demonstrations, and live music.
Seasonal Events:
* Holiday Festival of Lights: A magical holiday light display at James Island County Park.
* Charleston Greek Festival: A cultural celebration featuring Greek food, music, and dance.
* Charleston Greek Festival: A cultural celebration featuring Greek food, music, and dance.

Additional Tips:
* Check the Charleston CVB website for the most up-to-date information on festivals and events.
* Plan ahead: Popular festivals can sell out quickly, so it's best to book accommodations and tickets in advance.

* Embrace the local culture: Attend local festivals and events to experience the true spirit of Charleston.

By attending one of these festivals, you can immerse yourself in the vibrant culture of Charleston and create unforgettable memories.

Shopping

Charleston offers a diverse shopping experience, from historic markets to modern boutiques. Here are some of the best places to shop in Charleston:

Historic Shopping:

* Charleston City Market: This historic market is a great place to find local crafts, souvenirs, and fresh produce.

* King Street: This bustling street is lined with shops, boutiques, and art galleries.

Modern Shopping:

* The Shops at Charleston Place: This upscale shopping mall features high-end boutiques and department stores.

* Citadel Mall: This traditional mall offers a variety of stores, including department stores, clothing stores, and electronics stores.

* Tanger Outlets: This outlet mall offers great deals on brand-name clothing, shoes, and accessories.
Unique Boutiques:
* Hampden Clothing: This popular boutique offers stylish clothing and accessories for men and women.
* M. Dumas & Sons: This family-owned store has been selling fine men's clothing for over 100 years.

* Candlefish: This store offers a wide variety of candles, soaps, and other home goods.
Tips for Shopping in Charleston:
* Best Time to Shop: Spring and Fall are the best times to shop in Charleston, as the weather is mild and there are fewer crowds.
* Sales Tax: Charleston has a 7% sales tax.

* Bargaining: While bargaining is not common in Charleston, you may be able to negotiate prices at some of the smaller shops.

* Support Local Businesses: Consider shopping at local boutiques and markets to support the local economy.

By exploring the diverse shopping options in Charleston, you can find unique treasures and souvenirs to remember your trip.

Seafood

Charleston is renowned for its fresh seafood, and there are countless restaurants where you can savor delicious seafood dishes. Here are some of the top-rated seafood restaurants in Charleston:

Classic Seafood Restaurants:

* Hyman's Seafood: This iconic restaurant offers a wide variety of seafood dishes, from oysters and shrimp to crab cakes and lobster.

* Charleston Crab House: As the name suggests, this restaurant specializes in crab dishes, including crab cakes, crab dip, and crab legs.

* Hank's Seafood Restaurant: This popular restaurant serves classic Lowcountry seafood dishes, such as shrimp and grits and she-crab soup.

Modern Seafood Restaurants:
* Coast Bar & Grill: This trendy restaurant offers a modern take on classic seafood dishes, with a focus on fresh, local ingredients.

* Amen Street Fish + Raw Bar: This restaurant offers a variety of raw bar options, as well as cooked seafood dishes.

* The Watch Rooftop Kitchen & Spirits: This rooftop restaurant offers stunning views of the city and a delicious seafood menu.

Tips for Enjoying Seafood in Charleston:
* Try Lowcountry Cuisine: Lowcountry cuisine is a regional style of cooking that emphasizes fresh seafood, rice, and vegetables.

* Order Oysters: Charleston is known for its fresh oysters, which can be enjoyed raw, steamed, or fried.

* Pair with Local Beer or Wine: Many Charleston restaurants offer a selection of local beers and wines that complement seafood dishes.
 * Ask Your Server for Recommendations: Your server can help you choose the best dishes based on your preferences.
By exploring the diverse seafood scene in Charleston, you can experience the best of Lowcountry cuisine.

Dining
Charleston's dining scene is a vibrant mix of classic Southern cuisine and innovative modern flavors. Here are some of the top-rated restaurants in the city:
Fine Dining:
 * FIG: This Michelin-starred restaurant offers innovative dishes made with fresh, local ingredients.

* Husk: This James Beard Award-winning restaurant focuses on traditional Southern cuisine with a modern twist.
* Magnolias: This elegant restaurant serves classic Southern dishes in a beautiful setting.

Casual Dining:
* Hominy Grill: This popular restaurant serves up delicious Southern comfort food, including shrimp and grits and fried green tomatoes.
* Slightly North of Broad: This lively restaurant offers a diverse menu, including seafood, pasta, and steaks.
* The Ordinary: This seafood restaurant is known for its fresh oysters and other delicious seafood dishes.

Unique Dining Experiences:
* The Watch: This rooftop bar and restaurant offers stunning views of the city skyline and a delicious menu.
* Minero: This Mexican restaurant offers authentic Mexican cuisine with a modern twist.

* Kultura: This Filipino restaurant serves delicious and authentic Filipino dishes.

Tips for Dining in Charleston:
* Make Reservations: Popular restaurants can book up quickly, so it's best to make reservations in advance.
* Try Local Seafood: Charleston is known for its fresh seafood, so be sure to try some of the local specialties, such as shrimp and grits or she-crab soup.
* Pair Your Meal with a Local Beverage: Charleston has a thriving craft beer and cocktail scene, so be sure to try a local brew or a handcrafted cocktail.

* Don't Miss Dessert: Many restaurants in Charleston offer delicious desserts, such as sweet tea bread pudding and pecan pie.
By exploring the diverse dining scene in Charleston, you can experience the best of Southern cuisine and create unforgettable culinary memories.

For Kids

Here are some fun and engaging activities for kids in Charleston:

Interactive Fun:

 * Children's Museum of the Lowcountry: A hands-on museum with exhibits on science, art, and history.

 * South Carolina Aquarium: Explore marine life, touch stingrays, and learn about coastal ecosystems.

 * Adventure Sky Zone: Bounce around on trampolines, play dodgeball, and climb the walls at this indoor trampoline park.

 * Summit Adventure Park: Zipline through the trees, climb ropes courses, and test your balance on aerial bridges.

Outdoor Adventures:

 * Beaches: Enjoy swimming, sunbathing, and building sandcastles at Folly Beach, Sullivan's Island, or Isle of Palms.

 * Parks and Playgrounds: Visit Hampton Park, Marion Square, or Waterfront Park for picnics, playgrounds, and open spaces.

* Boating and Kayaking: Explore the waterways of Charleston Harbor on a guided tour or rent a kayak.
* Fort Sumter and Fort Moultrie: Learn about the history of these important military sites.

Cultural Experiences:
* Horse-Drawn Carriage Rides: Take a scenic ride through the historic district and learn about the city's history.
* Pirate Ship Adventure: Embark on a pirate adventure with treasure hunts, water battles, and storytelling.
* Charleston RiverDogs: Cheer on the local baseball team at a fun and family-friendly game.

Additional Tips:
* Plan Ahead: Check the websites of attractions and restaurants for hours of operation and special events.
* Pack Snacks and Water: Keep kids hydrated and happy with snacks and water.

* Dress Comfortably: Wear comfortable clothing and shoes, especially for outdoor activities.

* Use Sunscreen: Protect your kids' skin from the sun, especially during the summer months. By planning your trip and choosing activities that cater to your kids' interests, you can create unforgettable memories in Charleston.

Drinking

Charleston offers a vibrant nightlife scene with a variety of bars, pubs, and cocktail lounges. Here are some of the top spots to enjoy a drink in Charleston:

Cocktail Bars:

* The Gin Joint: This speakeasy-style bar offers a wide selection of classic and innovative cocktails.

* Prohibition: This upscale bar features a Prohibition-era theme and a creative cocktail menu.

* The Living Room at The Dewberry: This stylish bar offers a sophisticated atmosphere and a creative cocktail menu.

Beer Bars:
* Edmund's Oast: This brewery and restaurant offers a wide selection of craft beers, as well as delicious food.

* Revelry Brewing Company: This local brewery offers a variety of beers, from IPAs to stouts.

* The Belmont: This neighborhood bar offers a great selection of craft beers and a laid-back atmosphere.

Wine Bars:
* Bin 152: This wine bar offers a wide selection of wines, as well as small plates and charcuterie boards.
* The Alley: This cozy wine bar offers a curated selection of wines and a relaxed atmosphere.

Rooftop Bars:
 * The Watch: This rooftop bar offers stunning views of the city skyline and a creative cocktail menu.
 * Élevé: This rooftop bar at the Hotel Bennett offers panoramic views of the city and a sophisticated atmosphere.
Tips for Drinking in Charleston:
 * Drink Responsibly: Always drink responsibly and know your limits.
 * Designated Driver: Designate a driver or use a ride-sharing service.

* Local Laws: Be aware of local laws and regulations regarding alcohol consumption.
 * Enjoy the Atmosphere: Charleston's bars and pubs offer a variety of atmospheres, from laid-back to upscale.
 * Pair Drinks with Food: Many bars and restaurants offer delicious food pairings to complement your drinks.
By exploring the diverse drinking scene in Charleston, you can experience the city's vibrant nightlife and create unforgettable memories.

Entertainment

Charleston offers a variety of entertainment options for all ages and interests. Here are some of the top entertainment options in the city:

Live Music:

 * Music Farm: This popular venue hosts a variety of concerts throughout the year, featuring both local and national acts.

 * Charleston Pour House: This bar and music venue offers live music every night of the week.

 * The Commodore: This historic theater hosts a variety of live performances, including music, comedy, and theater.

Theater:

 * Dock Street Theatre: This historic theater offers a variety of plays and musicals throughout the year.

 * Charleston Stage: This professional theater company produces a variety of shows, including classic plays and original works.

Comedy:

* Black Fedora Comedy Mystery Theatre: This unique theater offers interactive comedy-mystery shows.

Nightlife:

* King Street: This bustling street is home to a variety of bars, clubs, and lounges.

* The Battery: This historic district is a great place to enjoy a drink with a view of the harbor.

* Shem Creek: This waterfront area in Mount Pleasant offers a variety of bars and restaurants with live music.

Additional Tips:

* Check local listings: Keep an eye on local newspapers, websites, and social media for the latest events and performances.

* Plan ahead: If you're attending a popular event, be sure to purchase tickets in advance.

* Dress comfortably: Dress comfortably, especially if you're attending a concert or other outdoor event.

* Enjoy the atmosphere: Charleston has a vibrant nightlife scene, so relax, have fun, and enjoy the experience.

By exploring the various entertainment options in Charleston, you can experience the city's vibrant culture and create unforgettable memories.

Views & Vistas

Charleston offers a variety of stunning views and vistas, from historic landmarks to natural beauty. Here are some of the best places to enjoy the city's scenery:

Waterfront Views:

 * The Battery: This historic seawall offers breathtaking views of Charleston Harbor, Fort Sumter, and the city skyline.

 * Waterfront Park: This picturesque park features a beautiful promenade, perfect for strolling and enjoying the harbor views.

 * Shem Creek: This charming waterfront area in Mount Pleasant offers stunning views of the marsh and the Cooper River.

 * Rooftop Bars: Many rooftop bars in Charleston offer panoramic views of the city, including The Watch and Élevé.

Historic Charm:

* Rainbow Row: This iconic row of colorful houses is a feast for the eyes.

* French Quarter: Wander through the charming streets of this historic neighborhood and admire the beautiful architecture.

* King Street: Stroll down this historic street and admire the beautiful buildings and shops.
Natural Beauty:
* Folly Beach: Enjoy stunning ocean views and sunsets on this popular beach.

* Sullivan's Island: Relax on the beach or explore the historic Fort Moultrie.

* Kiawah Island: This luxurious island offers pristine beaches, lush forests, and stunning golf courses.

* Middleton Place: This historic plantation features beautiful gardens and picturesque landscapes.

Additional Tips:
 * Best Time to Visit: Spring and Fall offer
pleasant weather and fewer crowds.
 * Golden Hour: For the best photo
opportunities, try to visit during the golden hour,
which is the hour before sunset.
 * Respectful Viewing: Be mindful of private
property and avoid trespassing.
 * Enjoy the Moment: Take a moment to
appreciate the beauty of Charleston and its
surroundings.
By exploring these locations, you can experience
the stunning beauty of Charleston and create
unforgettable memories.

For Free
Here are some of the best free things to do in
Charleston:
Explore the Historic District:
 * Stroll through Rainbow Row: Admire the
colorful houses and take photos.
 * Walk along The Battery: Enjoy the waterfront
views and historic architecture.

* Visit White Point Garden: Relax in this serene park and enjoy the beautiful scenery.

* Explore the French Quarter: Wander through the charming streets and admire the beautiful churches.
 * Window Shop on King Street: Take in the sights and sounds of this bustling shopping street.
Enjoy the Outdoors:
 * Visit Waterfront Park: Relax by the water, enjoy the fountain, and take in the views of the harbor.

 * Hike or Bike the Ravenel Bridge: Get some exercise and enjoy stunning views of the city.
 * Visit the Angel Oak Tree: Marvel at this ancient live oak tree on Johns Island.

 * Explore the Beaches: Spend a day at Folly Beach, Sullivan's Island, or Isle of Palms.
 * Picnic in a Park: Pack a picnic lunch and enjoy the outdoors at Hampton Park or Waterfront Park.

Cultural Experiences:
 * Attend a Free Concert: Check local listings
for free concerts and festivals.
 * Visit the Charleston City Market: Browse the
stalls and soak up the atmosphere.

 * Explore the College of Charleston Campus:
Admire the beautiful architecture and historic
buildings.
 * Visit the Circular Congregational Church
Cemetery: Explore this historic cemetery and
learn about Charleston's past.
Additional Tips:
 * Check Local Events: Many free events and
festivals take place throughout the year.

 * Bring a Camera: Capture the beauty of
Charleston's historic sites and natural scenery.
 * Wear Comfortable Shoes: You'll be doing a
lot of walking, so wear comfortable shoes.
 * Stay Hydrated: Bring plenty of water,
especially during the warmer months.

By taking advantage of these free activities, you can experience the best of Charleston without breaking the bank.

Museums

Charleston offers a variety of museums that delve into the city's rich history, art, and culture. Here are some of the top museums to explore: History and Culture:

 * The Charleston Museum: This oldest museum in the United States showcases the region's history, art, and natural history.

 * Old Slave Mart Museum: This poignant museum explores the history of slavery in Charleston.

 * International African American Museum: This museum tells the story of the African American experience, from slavery to the present day.

 * Gibbes Museum of Art: This museum features American art from the 18th century to the present.

* South Carolina Historical Society: This museum explores the history of South Carolina, with exhibits on the Civil War, the Revolutionary War, and more.

Maritime and Military:
* Patriots Point Naval & Maritime Museum: This museum features historic naval vessels, including the USS Yorktown aircraft carrier.

* Fort Sumter and Fort Moultrie: These historic forts played significant roles in American history.

Other Notable Museums:
* Children's Museum of the Lowcountry: A fun and interactive museum for kids.

* Nathaniel Russell House: This historic house museum offers a glimpse into the lives of 19th-century Charleston residents.

* Old Exchange and Provost Dungeon: This historic building was once a jail, a courthouse, and a post office.

By visiting these museums, you can gain a deeper understanding of Charleston's rich history and culture.

Escapes

Here are a few ideas for day trips and weekend getaways from Charleston:

Day Trips:

* Moncks Corner: This charming town offers a slower pace of life, with opportunities for fishing, kayaking, and exploring nature.

* Summerville: A historic town with beautiful antebellum homes, art galleries, and boutique shops.

* Isle of Palms: A barrier island with pristine beaches, perfect for swimming, sunbathing, and surfing.

* Folly Beach: A laid-back beach town with a vibrant surf culture and delicious seafood.

Weekend Getaways:
 * Myrtle Beach: A popular beach destination with amusement parks, golf courses, and endless shopping opportunities.
 * Asheville, North Carolina: A mountain town with a vibrant arts scene, breweries, and stunning natural beauty.
 * Savannah, Georgia: A historic city with beautiful squares, charming architecture, and delicious Southern cuisine.
 * Hilton Head Island: A luxurious island resort with championship golf courses, pristine beaches, and world-class spas.

Additional Tips:
 * Check the Weather: Before planning your trip, check the weather forecast to ensure optimal conditions for your chosen activities.
 * Pack Accordingly: Pack appropriate clothing and footwear for your chosen activities.
 * Plan Your Itinerary: Create a detailed itinerary to make the most of your time.
 * Book Accommodations in Advance: If you're planning a weekend getaway, book your

accommodations well in advance, especially during peak season.

By taking advantage of these nearby destinations, you can experience a variety of different landscapes, cultures, and activities.

Survival Guide

A Survival Guide to Charleston

Before You Go:

 * Pack for the Weather: Charleston's weather can be unpredictable, so pack for a range of temperatures. Light layers are ideal, especially during the spring and fall.

 * Research Accommodations: Book your accommodations in advance, especially during peak seasons. Consider the location, amenities, and budget.

* Plan Your Itinerary: Research attractions, restaurants, and activities you want to experience. A well-planned itinerary will help you make the most of your trip.

Arriving in Charleston:

* Airport: Charleston International Airport is the main airport serving the city.
* Transportation:
  * Rental Car: A car rental allows for flexibility to explore the city and surrounding areas.
  * Public Transportation: CARTA provides bus service within Charleston.
  * Ride-Sharing Services: Uber and Lyft are available.
  * Walking: The historic district is best explored on foot.

Getting Around:
* Walking: The historic district is pedestrian-friendly.
* Biking: Bike rentals are available for exploring the city.
* Car: A car provides flexibility for exploring the city and surrounding areas.
* Public Transportation: CARTA provides bus service within Charleston.

Essential Information:
* Currency: US Dollar

* Language: English
* Tipping: 15-20% tip is customary in restaurants.
* Emergency Number: 911
* Local Time: Eastern Standard Time (EST)
Safety Tips:
* Stay Aware: Be aware of your surroundings, especially at night.
* Secure Valuables: Keep valuables secure in a hotel safe or with you.
* Respect Local Customs: Dress modestly, especially when visiting historical sites and churches.

Behind the Scenes:
* Charleston's History: Learn about the city's rich history, including its role in the Civil War.
* Local Culture: Immerse yourself in the local culture by attending festivals, trying local cuisine, and listening to live music.
* Photography: Capture the beauty of Charleston's historic architecture, colorful streets, and stunning waterfront.

By following these tips, you can make the most of your trip to Charleston and have a memorable experience.

Before You Go
Before You Go: A Guide to Charleston
Packing:
 * Comfortable Shoes: Charleston's historic district is best explored on foot, so pack comfortable walking shoes.
 * Lightweight Clothing: Pack light, breathable clothing, especially during the warmer months.
 * Rain Gear: Charleston can be unpredictable, so a light rain jacket or umbrella is recommended.
 * Sunscreen and Hat: Protect yourself from the sun, especially during the summer months.
 * Camera: Capture the beauty of Charleston's historic architecture and stunning scenery.

Accommodation:
 * Historic District: Stay in the heart of the action and experience the city's charm.

* Beachfront: Enjoy the ocean breeze and stunning views at one of the many beachfront hotels.
 * Budget-Friendly: Consider staying in a nearby town like Mount Pleasant or North Charleston for more affordable options.

Transportation:
 * Walking: The historic district is best explored on foot.
 * Biking: Rent a bike to explore the city at your own pace.
 * Car Rental: A car allows for greater flexibility to explore the surrounding areas.
 * Public Transportation: CARTA provides bus service within Charleston.
 * Ride-Sharing Services: Uber and Lyft are available.

Local Customs and Etiquette:
 * Southern Hospitality: Charleston is known for its friendly and welcoming people.
 * Respectful Dress: Dress modestly, especially when visiting churches and historical sites.

* Tipping: Tipping is customary in restaurants and for services like taxis and tours.

Budgeting:
 * Accommodation: Budget for a variety of accommodations, from budget-friendly hotels to luxury resorts.
 * Food: Charleston has a diverse culinary scene, with options for all budgets.
 * Activities: Many attractions offer free admission or discounted rates.
 * Transportation: Consider the cost of transportation, whether it's renting a car, using public transportation, or walking.
By planning ahead and considering these tips, you can make the most of your trip to Charleston.

Arriving in Charleston
Arriving in Charleston: A Smooth Landing
By Air:
 * Charleston International Airport (CHS): This is the primary airport serving Charleston. Upon arrival, you'll find rental car agencies, taxis, ride-

sharing services, and public transportation options.

By Car:

 * Interstate Highways: Interstates 26 and 526 lead directly into Charleston.

 * Scenic Routes: Consider taking a more scenic route along the coast or through the

Lowcountry.

Upon Arrival:

 * Transportation:

   * Rental Car: Convenient for exploring the city and surrounding areas.

   * Taxi: A reliable option, especially for shorter distances.

   * Ride-Sharing Services: Uber and Lyft are available in Charleston.

   * Public Transportation: CARTA provides bus service within the city.

 * Currency: The US Dollar is the currency used in Charleston.

 * Time Zone: Eastern Standard Time (EST)

 * Local Customs: Charleston is known for its Southern hospitality, so be polite and courteous.

* Emergency Number: 911
Getting Oriented:
 * Historic District: This is the heart of Charleston and a great place to start your exploration.
 * Waterfront: The waterfront offers stunning views of the harbor and is a popular spot for walks and dining.
 * Neighborhoods: Charleston has various neighborhoods, each with its own unique charm. By following these tips, you can ensure a smooth arrival and a memorable stay in Charleston.

Getting Around

Here are the best ways to get around Charleston:
Walking:
 * Best for: Exploring the historic district, shopping on King Street, and visiting nearby attractions.
 * Benefits: Free, healthy, and allows you to immerse yourself in the city's atmosphere.

Biking:
 * Best for: Covering more ground quickly and enjoying the fresh air.
 * Benefits: Numerous bike rental shops are available throughout the city.
 * Consider: Bike lanes can be limited in some areas, so be cautious.
CARTA (Charleston Area Regional

Transportation Authority):
 * Best for: Getting to and from the airport, exploring different neighborhoods, and commuting to work or school.
 * Benefits: Affordable and environmentally friendly.
 * Consider: Limited routes and schedules, especially on weekends and evenings.

Ride-sharing Services:
 * Best for: Door-to-door transportation, especially at night or in less walkable areas.
 * Benefits: Convenient and affordable.
 * Consider: Surge pricing during peak times and limited availability in certain areas.

Taxis:
* Best for: Quick and direct transportation, especially for short distances.
* Benefits: Available 24/7.
* Consider: Can be more expensive than ride-sharing services, especially for longer distances.

Car Rental:
* Best for: Exploring the surrounding areas, such as Folly Beach, Sullivan's Island, and Kiawah Island.
* Benefits: Flexibility and convenience.
* Consider: Parking can be challenging in the historic district, and traffic can be heavy during peak times.

Additional Tips:
* Plan your route: Use a map or navigation app to plan your route and avoid traffic congestion.
* Be aware of traffic patterns: Traffic can be heavy during peak times, especially in the summer.

* Respect pedestrians and cyclists: Share the road and be mindful of others.

* Check for parking: Many attractions and restaurants have limited parking, so consider alternative transportation options.

By considering these options and planning accordingly, you can easily navigate Charleston and make the most of your trip.

Essential Information

Essential Information for Your Charleston Trip

Contact Information

Charleston Area Convention & Visitors Bureau (CVB):

 * Website: charlestoncvb.com
 * Phone: (843) 853-8000
 * Email: [charlestoninanutshell@gmail.com]
 * Address: 205 Meeting Street, Charleston, SC 29401

Emergency Numbers
 * Police: 911
 * Fire: 911
 * Ambulance: 911

Currency
 * US Dollar is the official currency.

Language
 * English is the primary language spoken.

Time Zone
 * Eastern Standard Time (EST)

Electrical Outlets
 * Type A and B: Standard US plugs.

Tipping
 * Restaurants: 15-20% tip is customary.
 * Bars: A dollar or two per drink is standard.
 * Taxis and Rideshares: 15-20% tip is common.

Local Customs
 * Southern Hospitality: Locals are known for their friendly and welcoming nature.
 * Sweet Tea: A Southern staple, often served iced.
 * Lowcountry Cuisine: Try local delicacies like shrimp and grits, she-crab soup, and boiled peanuts.
 * Historical Significance: Respect the city's rich history and heritage.
By keeping these essential details in mind, you can ensure a smooth and enjoyable trip to Charleston.

Language

The primary language spoken in Charleston, South Carolina, is English. However, the city's rich history and diverse cultural influences have led to the development of unique dialects and languages.

Gullah-Geechee: This is a distinct language spoken by the Gullah-Geechee people, an African American population living in the coastal regions of South Carolina and Georgia. It's a creole language with roots in English and various

African languages.

Spanish: Due to recent immigration trends, Spanish is becoming increasingly common in Charleston, particularly in certain neighborhoods.

While these languages add to the cultural richness of Charleston, English remains the dominant language used for business, tourism, and everyday interactions.

Behind the Scenes
Behind the Scenes of Charleston's Charm

A Glimpse into the Historic City
Charleston, often referred to as the "Holy City,"
is a place steeped in history and culture. Behind
its picturesque façade lies a rich tapestry of
stories, traditions, and challenges that have
shaped the city into what it is today.

Preserving the Past:
 * Historic Preservation: Charleston is renowned
for its commitment to historic preservation.
Strict regulations govern the restoration and
maintenance of historic buildings, ensuring that
the city's unique character is preserved for future
generations.

 * The Preservation Society of Charleston: This
organization plays a crucial role in safeguarding
Charleston's heritage. They work to protect
historic buildings, promote public awareness of
the city's history, and advocate for responsible
development.
The Gullah-Geechee Culture:
 * A Unique Heritage: The Gullah-Geechee
people, descendants of enslaved Africans, have a

rich cultural heritage that has significantly influenced Charleston's cuisine, music, and art.
 * Preserving Traditions: Efforts are being made to preserve Gullah-Geechee culture through festivals, heritage organizations, and educational programs.

Modern Challenges:
 * Tourism and Development: While tourism is a major economic driver, it also presents challenges such as overcrowding, traffic congestion, and the erosion of local culture.
 * Climate Change: Rising sea levels and increasingly frequent hurricanes pose significant threats to Charleston's coastal environment and infrastructure.

 * Affordable Housing: As Charleston becomes an increasingly popular destination, the demand for housing has led to rising prices and displacement of long-time residents.
Despite these challenges, Charleston remains a vibrant and captivating city. By understanding the forces that shape its past, present, and future,

visitors can appreciate the city's unique character and contribute to its ongoing preservation.

Made in the USA
Middletown, DE
16 May 2025